Hanna-Jane's Darling, Gorgeous Cat

Elizabeth Eberstein

In loving memory of Lucifer.

My name is Hanna-Jane and I would like to tell you about my darling, gorgeous cat, Lucifer. Mummy already had Lucifer when I was born. He was part of my family and my special playmate.

The first thing Mummy taught me was to be kind to animals. Even before I could walk, Mummy taught me to be very gentle with Lucifer. She made sure I did not pull his tail or pull his fur or pinch him or things like that.

Mummy said, "It's no wonder children who are cruel to cats get scratched or bitten. It is their own fault if they get hurt. If you are nice to cats they will be nice to you."

Lucifer was a very patient cat. Sometimes he let me dress him. He looked so funny. One day, I put a hat on his head and put him on Mummy's bed. When Mummy woke up, there was a cat with a hat on her bed. It was so funny. Mummy and I laughed and laughed.

Lucifer was such good fun to play with. We played pretend games together all the time. When I played mothers and fathers, Lucifer was my baby. When I took my dolls to pretend childcare, Lucifer had to come, too. One Christmas, I even put him in a shopping bag and pretended he was my Christmas present. Lucifer was so cool.

Sadly, when I was five years old, Lucifer became very sick. Mummy took him to the vet. The vet said Lucifer would not get better. He was a very old cat. His lungs were no longer working very well. They would not work for very much longer. Mummy told me Lucifer would die if he could not breathe.

Lucifer had an operation to help him breathe.

After that, Mummy often had to take him to the vet. Poor Lucifer was not very well at all. He could hardly breathe and was in a lot of pain. One day, Mummy said it was time for the vet to give Lucifer a needle to put him to sleep. Mummy said he would not wake up anymore. Everyone came to say "Goodbye" to Lucifer. I gave him a nice cuddle and a pat.

I was very sad because I wouldn't have Lucifer to play with anymore. Mummy and I cried. Daddy stayed with me while Mummy took Lucifer to the vet.

Mummy brought Lucifer home after the vet put him to sleep. We made a bed in a box. We put Lucifer and his favourite toy in the box. It was a fishing line with a furry toy fish on it. I also did a drawing for Lucifer and we put that in the box, too.

Then, that day in the afternoon, we buried him under his favourite tree. We put some rocks on the grave and we lit a candle on the rocks. We were very sad. Lucifer was such a good cat. I wished he did not have to die until he was 100 years old. Then I could have had him for my whole life.

I asked my Omi what would happen to Lucifer now. She is my German Grandmother.

Omi said, "I don't know. I'd like to think that Lucifer will go to a happy place."

"Omi," I said, "when we buried Lucifer, I saw a beautiful rainbow. Do you think Lucifer went to his new place on the rainbow?"

"That would be nice, Hanna-Jane," Omi replied. "Some people think cats have nine lives. Maybe he will come back as a little black kitten." Omi gave me a big hug.

The next day Omi and I went to a big hardware store. The store was having a celebration and Omi bought me a sausage. A lady was doing face painting. I told her about Lucifer and I asked her to paint my face like a black cat.

I thought Lucifer would have liked that. I went to sleep that night with my face painted like a black cat. Then, the next day, I went to school with my face painted. I told the teacher about my cat. She let me wear my cat face all day. Then I washed it off.

After Lucifer died, my Aunty in Germany sent me a toy elephant. I called her Elli. I took her everywhere. I took her to bed, too. She was nice to cuddle, just like Lucifer.

One day, I pretended to row to Bruny Island in my cardboard boat. I took all my provisions in another cardboard boat. I even took Elli. I put her under the blanket to keep her warm. Daddy was watching. He said, "Hanna-Jane, don't you think an elephant is a bit heavy to go into your small boat. You will sink, won't you?"

"But she wants to come," I said.

When we nearly got to Bruny Island, the boat sank and Elli and I had to swim ashore. Of course, what really happened is that the cardboard box accidentally fell over and Elli and I fell out.

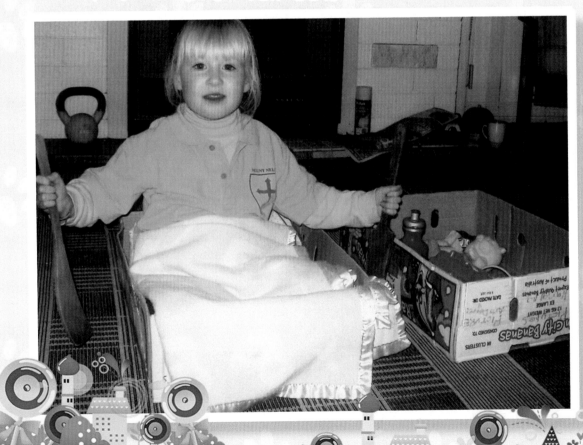

Daddy laughed and said, "I told you so". I missed Lucifer very much. If I had been able to take Lucifer instead of Elli, I am sure we would not have fallen out of our pretend boat. Everything was more fun when I had Lucifer to play with.

I asked Daddy if we could have a little black kitten. When it grew up it would look just like Lucifer. Daddy said, maybe I should not talk about that to Mummy just yet because she was still very upset about Lucifer's death.

But I did ask Mummy if we could get a kitten. Mummy said, "One day, not just now. I need time to get used to Lucifer not living at our house anymore." Daddy was right.

A long time passed. I had my sixth birthday. I like being six. I can do many things by myself now. I can even tie the laces of my black school shoes. I had to practice for a long time before I could do that. Mummy and Daddy always say that if I can't do something, I have to ask for help. But first, I have to try very, very hard to do it myself. Mummy says that is how children become "independent". That means you don't have to have everyone do things for you like a baby. I still miss Lucifer, especially when I come home from school. He used to sit on a tree stump and wait for me every day.

One day, when I was having fun playing with Daddy's red hat, I heard the telephone ring. It was the vet who had put Lucifer to sleep.

He said, "I have a black kitten that needs a home. Would you like to have him?"
"Please, please, please, Mummy, say 'yes'!" I pleaded.

And guess what? Mummy said we could have the kitten! So now, we have another cat to love and look after. Of course, we will always remember Lucifer. I still put flowers on his grave.

I also painted a picture of Lucifer on a rainbow. I hung it on my bedroom wall. Every time I look at it, I think about Lucifer.

I called the new kitten Toby.

I used to look after a puppy called Toby. But I had to give him away because he was going to become a guide dog for a blind person. So I called the kitten Toby Two. And my Toby is not going away. He is going to stay with us forever and ever.

Printed in the United States
By Bookmasters